101 REASONS WHY YOU SUCK AT GOLF

JACK FENN

ISBN: 978-1-962496-09-4

For questions, please reach out to Support@OakHarborPress.com

Please consider leaving a review!

Just visit: OakHarborPress.com/Reviews

FREE BONUS

SCAN ME!

GET OUR NEXT BOOK FOR FREE!
Scan or go to:
OakHarborPress.com/Free

TABLE OF CONTENTS

[1]
THINKING "BIRDIE" IS A CHARACTER FROM SESAME STREET

[2]
BELIEVING SAND TRAPS ARE FOR BUILDING CASTLES

[3]
USING GPS TO FIND THE HOLE

[4]
YOUR IDEA OF A "SWING" IS ON A PLAYGROUND

[5]
YOU CONSIDER USING A METAL DETECTOR TO FIND YOUR BALL

[6]
YOUR PUTTER SPENDS MORE TIME AIRBORNE THAN YOUR BALLS

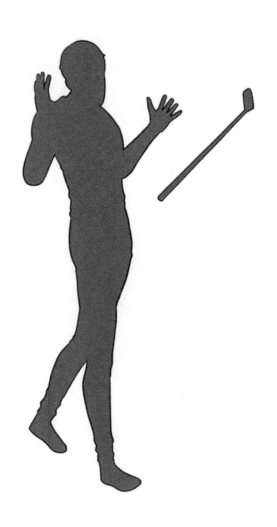

[7]
YOUR GOLF CART RUNS OUT OF BATTERY MORE OFTEN THAN YOUR PHONE

[8]
THINKING THE "19TH HOLE" IS A PRACTICE ROUND

[9]
THE DUCKS RUN *TOWARDS* THE WATER WHEN YOU'RE UP

[10]
BELIEVING GOLF GLOVES ARE FOR PUPPET SHOWS

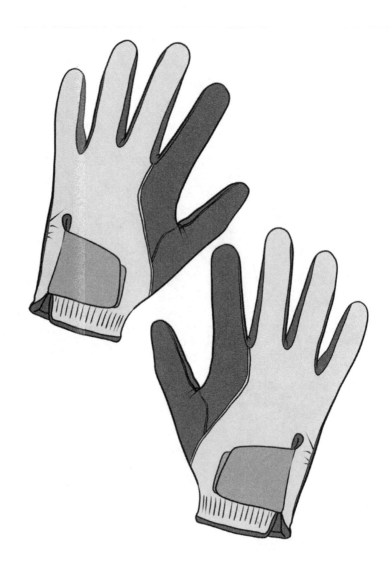

[11]
THINKING A "DRIVE" IS HEADING TO THE CLUBHOUSE

[12]
YOU'VE USED A POOL NOODLE AS A CLUB

[13]
YOUR SCORECARD RESEMBLES ADVANCED CALCULUS

[14]
YOU'VE SEARCHED FOR YOUR BALL ... IN THE PARKING LOT

[15]
YOUR BACKSWING LOOKS LIKE INTERPRETIVE DANCE

[16]
ASKING IF THE COURSE HAS A "MULLIGAN" LOYALTY CARD

[17]
YOUR CADDIE APPLIED FOR HAZARD PAY

[18]
YOU'VE ATTEMPTED TO TEE OFF WITH A BASEBALL BAT

[19]
YOUR "SLICE" ISN'T A PIZZA ORDER

[20]
"FORE!" IS THE NUMBER OF BALLS LOST ON YOUR LAST HOLE

[21]
YOU BRING A FLASK FOR CONFIDENCE

[22]
HAVING A STRONGER RELATIONSHIP WITH THE BUNKER RAKES THAN YOUR CLUBS

[23]
YOU TAKE MORE SHOTS THAN A CAMERA CREW

[24]
YOUR WARDROBE IS LOUDER THAN YOUR SWING

[25]
YOU ONLY OWN A DRIVER

[26]
YOUR GOLF GAME LOOKS MORE LIKE YOGA PRACTICE

[27]
YOU'VE INTERRUPTED A PICNIC TO PLAY THROUGH

[28]
YOUR IDEA OF WATER HAZARD IS SPILLING YOUR DRINK

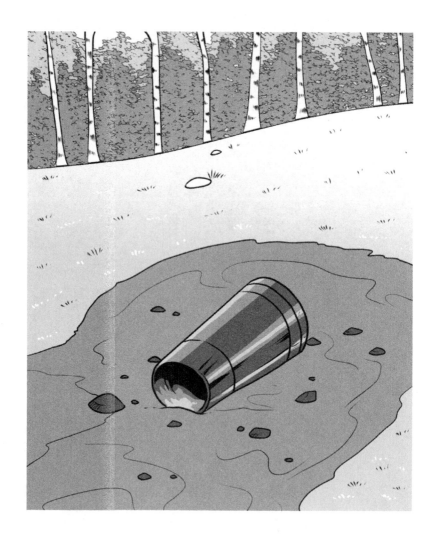

[29]
TREES MAGNETICALLY ATTRACT YOUR BALLS

[30]
YOUR BALLS SPEND MORE TIME IN THE WOODS THAN A PARK RANGER

[31]
SQUIRRELS HAVE STARTED COLLECTING YOUR BALLS AS WINTER PROVISIONS

[32]
YOU THOUGHT "PAR" WAS THE NUMBER OF STROKES ON THE FIRST HOLE

[33]
YOUR WEDGE HAS DUG MORE

[34]
YOU ONCE TRIED PLAYING IN FLIP-FLOPS

[35]
YOU'VE GOTTEN MORE EXERCISE CHASING THE BEVERAGE CART THAN SWINGING A CLUB

[36]
YOU'VE ASKED IF THE HOLES GET BIGGER AFTER 5 P.M.

[37]
YOU HIT A SAND WEDGE ...
FROM A GREENSIDE

[38]
YOUR GOLF BAG
IS JUST A FANCY
PICNIC BASKET

[39]
YOU BRING MORE SNACKS THAN BALLS

[40]
YOUR IDEA OF A "HOOK" IS A CATCHY SONG

[41]
YOU'VE TAKEN A
SELFIE MID-SWING

[42]
YOU'VE USED THE TERM "CLOSE ENOUGH" FOR BALLS 10 FEET FROM THE HOLE

[43]
YOU'VE ASKED FOR A COURSE MAP—AND A TRANSLATOR

[44]
THE SOUND OF YOUR SWING IS OFTEN FOLLOWED BY "OOPS!"

[45]
YOUR CLUB CHOICE IS BASED ON ITS COLOR

[46]
YOUR GOLF BALLS HAVE AN EXPIRATION DATE

[47]
THE PRO SHOP HAS A "LOST AND FOUND" BIN JUST FOR YOU

[48]
YOU'VE WONDERED WHY GOLF BALLS AREN'T MADE TO FLOAT

[49]
YOU THINK BOGEY IS A MONSTER'S NAME

[50]
YOUR FAVORITE CLUB IS A SANDWICH

[51]
YOU'VE ASKED IF THE GREENS COME IN ANOTHER COLOR

[52]
YOU'VE TRIED BRIBING THE COURSE FOR A BETTER SCORE

[53]
YOU THINK CLUBS SHOULD COME WITH TRAINING WHEELS

[54]
YOU'VE HAD MORE LESSONS THAN A KINDERGARTEN CLASS

[55]
YOU BELIEVE SUNSCREEN DOUBLES AS GRIP ENHANCER

[56]
YOUR SWING'S GOT RHYTHM—JUST NOT THE RIGHT ONE

[57]
YOU'VE TRIED USING A MAGIC 8-BALL TO DECIDE YOUR NEXT SHOT

[58]
YOU'VE ASKED IF THE COURSE HAS A BALL RENTAL CENTER

[59]
YOU'VE LOOKED UP "HOW TO WIN AT GOLF — WITHOUT PLAYING"

[60]
YOU CONSIDER ANY ROUND UNDER 150 A PERSONAL BEST

[61]
YOU'VE MISTOOK THE BALL CLEANER FOR A DRINK DISPENSER

[62]
YOUR FAVORITE CLUB IS THE 3-WOOD — FOR ITS MUSICAL SOUND

[63]
YOU THINK EVERY ROUND IS JUST A PRACTICE ROUND

[64]
YOU'VE THROWN YOUR CLUBS IN A RAGE

[65]
YOU'VE WONDERED WHY THERE ISN'T A GOLF BALL DRONE RETRIEVAL SERVICE

[66]
THE LOCAL BIRDS HAVE SET UP AN EARLY WARNING SYSTEM

[67]
YOU'VE WORN A HELMET —
JUST IN CASE

[68]
YOU THINK "DUFFER" IS YOUR NICKNAME

[69]
YOUR SHADOW HAS PLAYED BETTER THAN YOU

[70]
YOU'VE CONDUCTED AN INTERNET SEARCH FOR "HOW TO HIT A GOLF BALL"

[71]
YOU'VE WORN THE GREEN OUT — WITH FRUSTRATION

[72]
YOUR PEP TALK IS "DON'T HIT THE CARS"

[73]
YOU THINK BIRDIES, EAGLES, AND ALBATROSSES ARE PART OF A WILDLIFE SPOTTING GAME

[74]
YOUR CLUBS HAVE SEEN
MORE WATER THAN FISH

[75]
YOUR STRATEGY IS HOPE

[76]
YOU BELIEVE GOLF TEES ARE FOR MAKING MINI SCULPTURES

[77]
YOU'VE TRIED USING A MALLET

[78]
YOU'VE HIT MORE SPECTATORS THAN FAIRWAYS

[79]
THE COURSE FISH KNOW
YOU BY NAME

[80]
YOU'VE ASKED IF THERE'S A "FIND MY GOLF BALL" APP

[81]
YOU BRING EXTRA BALLS. NOT FOR THE WATER, BUT THE SKY.

[82]
YOU THINK GREENKEEPERS PLANT TREES JUST TO ANNOY YOU

[83]
YOU'VE INQUIRED IF THE DRIVING RANGE DELIVERS

[84]
YOUR PLAYLIST IS LOUDER THAN YOUR FOCUS

[85]
YOU'VE TRIED SETTING THE COURSE TO "EASY MODE"

[86]
YOU'VE WONDERED IF GOLF WOULD BE EASIER WITH A TENNIS RACKET

[87]
YOUR SWING HAS BEEN DESCRIBED AS "AVANT-GARDE"

[88]
YOU'VE TRIED NEGOTIATING WITH THE HOLE

[89]
YOUR FRIENDS STARTED CALLING YOU "WHIFF"

[90]
YOUR SWING HAS BEEN DESCRIBED AS "AVANT-GARDE"

[91]
YOU'VE TRIED NEGOTIATING WITH THE HOLE

[92]
YOUR CLUBS HAVE MORE EMOTIONAL BAGGAGE THAN AN AIRPORT TERMINAL

[93]
THE SUN GLARE IS ALWAYS YOUR EXCUSE — EVEN ON CLOUDY DAYS

[94]
YOU'VE GIVEN EACH OF YOUR BALLS A PEP TALK BEFORE TEEING OFF

[95]
YOU ONCE BROUGHT A STEP LADDER TO SEE OVER A BUNKER

[96]
YOU THINK WEARING TWO GLOVES DOUBLES YOUR GRIP

[97]
YOU'VE PUTTED — FROM THE TEE BOX

[98]
YOUR GOLF CART HAS ITS OWN FREQUENT FLYER MILES

[99]
YOU'VE EARNESTLY ASKED IF MINI-GOLF COUNTS TOWARDS YOUR HANDICAP

[100]
YOU BRING AN EXTRA SET OF CLOTHES — BECAUSE OF THE SAND TRAPS

[101]
YOUR "HOLE-IN-ONE" STORY INVOLVES A SQUIRREL, TWO DUCKS, AND A VERY CONFUSED FROG

Printed in Great Britain
by Amazon

34704567R00066